7/07

More Saints
Lives
& Illuminations

Ruth Sanderson

Eerdmans Books for Young Readers

Grand Rapids, Michigan • Cambridge, U.K.

This book is dedicated to Saint Patrick's Parish of Monson, Massachusetts
— *R. S.*

Text © 2007 Ruth Sanderson
Illustrations © 2007 Ruth Sanderson
Published in 2007 by Eerdmans Books for Young Readers,
an imprint of Wm. B. Eerdmans Publishing Co.

Wm. B. Eerdmans Publishing Co.
2140 Oak Industrial Dr. N.E., Grand Rapids, Michigan 49505
P.O. Box 163, Cambridge CB3 9PU U.K.

www.eerdmans.com/youngreaders

Manufactured in China

07 08 09 10 11   8 7 6 5 4 3 2 1

Library of Congress Cataloging-in-Publication Data

Sanderson, Ruth.
More Saints : lives and illuminations / written and illustrated by Ruth Sanderson.
p. cm.
ISBN 978-0-8028-5272-4 (alk. paper)
1. Christian saints — Biography. I. Title.
BX4655.3.S26 2006
282'.092'2 — dc22

2004010304

Text type set in Venetian
Illustrations created with pencils and oils
Gayle Brown, Art Director
Matthew Van Zomeren, Graphic Designer

Introduction

Becoming a saint isn't easy. Since the tenth century, the Roman Catholic Church has been using the same method of canonization, or declaring someone a saint. The process begins after the death of someone whom people regarded as holy. Many church leaders must approve the teachings and actions of the candidate before the pope will proclaim the person "venerable."

Unless the candidate was martyred, the next step in becoming a saint requires evidence of one miracle that must have occurred after the candidate's death. The candidate is then beatified, or declared "blessed" by the Church. At this time, the candidate can be adored by a particular group with whom the person holds special importance, and named as a group's patron. Only after more than one miracle can a pope canonize the person as a saint.

With words and pictures this book introduces thirty-four saints and two blesseds. Accompanying the full color illustration of each saint, you will find his or her dates of birth and death, feast day, biographical description, and patronage. A short glossary is included on page 40 to help with terms that may be unfamiliar.

While some elements of the saints' lives have been recorded by historians, other accounts have simply been passed down through generations, making it sometimes difficult to determine what is fact and what is legend. One thing is clear: these remarkable men and women still have the power to inspire us today.

Additional Resources

Books

Armstrong, Carole. *Lives and Legends of the Saints with Paintings from the Great Art Museums of the World.* (Simon & Schuster)

Ellsberg, Robert. *All Saints.* (CrossRoad Publishing)

Mornin, Edward and Lorna. *Saints: A Visual Guide.* (Eerdmans)

Llewellyn, Claire. *Saints and Angels.* (Houghton Mifflin)

Lovasik, Rev. Lawrence G. *New Picture Book of Saints: Illustrated Lives of the Saints for Young and Old.* (Catholic Book Publishing)

Websites

www.newadvent.org
www.catholic-forum.com
www.catholic.org

Saint Margaret of Scotland

1045–1093
NOVEMBER 16

Margaret, an English princess, was forced to flee her country when the Normans conquered in 1066. The conquerors sought to kill anyone with royal Saxon blood.

The princess took refuge at the court of King Malcolm of Scotland. After a few years, the king and Margaret married, and Margaret was crowned Queen of Scotland.

Margaret had two daughters and six sons, but her love and devotion extended to all the people of Scotland. She offered hospitality to anyone who needed it, especially to the poor, widows, orphans, and travelers. Every night Margaret invited several dozen beggars to eat at the castle. She would not sit down to eat until she had served the guests and washed their feet. By her virtuous example, the king's court became more civilized.

Margaret also tended to the spiritual needs of the people. She sent educated pastors around the country to reform corrupt practices in local churches. She commissioned the building of new churches, monasteries, and hostels for travelers.

In 1093 Margaret's husband and son were killed while defending their castle. Margaret died just four days later, on the very day she had predicted. She was canonized in 1251.

One of the queen's prized possessions was an illuminated pocket Bible, which miraculously remained in perfect condition after falling in a stream. It survives to this day and can be seen in a collection at Oxford University.

Patroness: Scotland, queens, widows, learning

Saint Isidore the Farmer

1070–1130

May 15

Isidore was a simple peasant who lived in Madrid, Spain. He married a poor girl named (Saint) Maria de la Cabeza, and the couple pledged to serve God faithfully. Isidore and Maria shared with those less fortunate than themselves and became models of Christian charity and virtue in their community.

Isidore worked for a rich farmer and arrived late to work every morning because he attended Mass. One day, his employer took him aside to complain. Isidore explained that the spiritual rewards he experienced at Mass allowed him to work more diligently for the rest of the day. His employer was not satisfied with this answer and secretly followed Isidore after church the next day.

According to legend, the rich farmer watched as Isidore hitched a team of oxen to a plow and began to work. His suspicion became awe when he saw another plow pulled by a pair of shining white oxen in the field beyond Isidore. When the rich man ran up to get a closer look, the oxen and plow disappeared. Word soon spread that Isidore's faith was so great that angels helped him work.

Another story tells how Isidore poured out half a sack of grain for a flock of hungry birds. When Isidore arrived at the mill to grind the grain, the sack was miraculously full again, and yielded double the amount of flour.

Many miracles were attributed to Isidore after his death — a king even declared he was cured of a serious illness as a result of Isidore's intercession. Isidore was canonized in 1622.

Patron: farmers, laborers, Madrid

Saint Bernard of Clairvaux

1090–1153
AUGUST 20

Bernard was born into a noble family in France and became a monk at the age of twenty-two. He was persuasive and charismatic, convincing thirty relatives and friends to join him at a poverty-stricken monastery at Cîteaux. Under his influence, the whole order was transformed.

In just a few years' time, Bernard was appointed abbot of a new monastery, where he served for the next thirty-eight years. He was devoted to the human lives of Jesus and the Blessed Virgin, and encouraged mystical prayer as part of the daily rule for his monks. In his lifetime several hundred monasteries were opened, and the number of monks at Clairvaux alone increased to seven hundred.

One of Bernard's students went on to become Pope Eugenius III. The pope approved Bernard's rule for a new order, the Knights Templar, who were dedicated to the Crusades and the care of pilgrims and others in need. After preaching support for a Crusade at the pope's request, Bernard was then blamed when the Crusade ended in looting and pillage. He in turn blamed the Crusaders for their sinful ways.

Throughout his lifetime, Bernard was known for his gift of miraculous healing. He also was regarded as such a powerful and eloquent preacher that he was sometimes called "mellifluous doctor" (literally, "the honey doctor") for his soothing and sweet voice. According to one story, his preaching skills were divinely bestowed by the Virgin Mary, who fed Bernard with her own milk. Bernard was canonized in 1174 and named a Doctor of the Church in 1830.

Patron: beekeepers, candle makers, Gibraltar

Saint Thomas Becket

1118–1170
DECEMBER 29

Thomas was born in England and was well educated from a young age. He attended the University of Paris and returned home to work as a clerk in the Archbishop of Canterbury's office. Archbishop Theobald was so impressed by Thomas's abilities that he took Thomas into his personal service and sent him abroad to study law.

After he finished his studies, Thomas was ordained and named Archdeacon of Canterbury. He became close friends with the new young king, Henry II, who appointed Thomas to rule as Chancellor of England. Thomas served Henry faithfully as a diplomat, a statesman and advisor, and a soldier. He dressed in opulent clothing, yet none could fault his character, and the country improved under his rule.

Everything changed when the king promoted Thomas again. As Archbishop of Canterbury, Thomas's duty was to serve the Church first, then the king. Thomas took his job seriously — he put aside his regal clothing and adopted the simple habit of a monk. This caused years of bitter disagreement and controversy over issues of Church and State between Thomas and the king. Matters escalated and Thomas's life was threatened. He was forced to flee to France. Several years later, upon his return to England, Thomas was assassinated by knights who claimed to be carrying out orders from King Henry.

Immediately after his death, Thomas was regarded as a martyr in defending the Church against secular powers. Many miracles were reported at his tomb, and he was canonized less than three years later.

Patron: clergy; Exeter College, Oxford

Saint Dominic

1170–1221
AUGUST 8

According to legend, Dominic's mother had a dream before he was born that she was carrying in her womb a dog holding a flaming torch that would set the world on fire. The Dominican order would later take this symbol to represent their mission to carry the light of the gospel into the world.

Dominic followed in the footsteps of his two older brothers and became a priest. During a trip to Rome he saw that Church authorities were failing to stop a group of heretics known as Albigenses, and he was inspired to join in the spiritual battle.

He believed the best way to convert heretics was simple: to preach the gospel. Dominic received permission from the pope to found the first order of monks dedicated to preaching, who became known as the Dominicans. Founded on the principles of prayer, study, ministry, and community, the Dominicans were dedicated to winning back all heretics, including the Albigenses, to the Church.

The pope led a Crusade, or holy war, against the Albigenses after a high-ranking Church official was murdered. Dominic did not agree with using force against heretics because thousands of people would be killed instead of being given the opportunity to convert.

One legend claims that Dominic became discouraged in the fight against the heretics until he received a vision from the Blessed Virgin. She gave him a wreath of roses and told him to say the rosary every day and to teach it to anyone who would listen. Thus, Dominic is sometimes credited for the invention of the rosary, though in fact this practice predates him.

Dominic died at age fifty-one and was canonized thirteen years after his death.

Patron: astronomers, scientists, the Dominican Republic

Saint Anthony of Padua

1195–1231
JUNE 13

Anthony was born in Lisbon, Portugal, and became an Augustinian monk when he was fifteen. But after he learned about the sacrifice of five Franciscan monks martyred for their faith, he left his order and joined the Franciscans in hopes of becoming a martyr himself.

He traveled to Morocco to witness, but became ill after several months and had to return home. He never arrived. Shipwrecked in Sicily, Italy, Anthony was nursed back to health by friars in the area. He lived in seclusion, leaving only to attend Mass and to sweep a nearby monastery.

When a scheduled speaker failed to appear at the monastery, Anthony was asked to give a short sermon. He astonished everyone with his eloquence, and soon thereafter began traveling, preaching, and teaching throughout the country.

There are many legends about Anthony's life. According to one, Anthony's gift of speech was so powerful that when he preached at a riverbank, the fish popped their heads out of the water to listen. Another legend claims Anthony's heart was so pure that the Christ Child himself appeared and kissed Anthony on the cheek.

Anthony spent the last years of his life in the city of Padua, where he preached his famous Lenten sermons. Many thousands of people crowded to hear him preach, so he often spoke outside. In fact, Anthony was so popular that he required a bodyguard to protect him from people who wanted to cut off a piece of his clothing as a relic.

So many miracles were attributed to Anthony's intercession that he was canonized a year after his death. He became a Doctor of the Church in 1946.

Patron: Padua, shipwrecks, married couples, children, travelers, retrieval of lost articles

Saint Francis of Assisi

1181–1226

OCTOBER 4

Born to a cloth merchant and a noblewoman, Francis lived in a wealthy home until his early twenties. One day, while praying in a run-down church, Francis heard a voice commanding, "Repair my house." Francis was so moved that he sold a bolt of his father's cloth to pay for restorations. His father found out and became furious, so Francis fled to a nearby cave.

When he returned to town a month later, Francis was a changed man. Barefoot and penniless, he adopted a simple lifestyle of charity and prayer, and lived as a beggar. Many people thought Francis was a madman, and his family disowned him.

Nevertheless, Francis became a roaming preacher and soon attracted a dozen followers. Eventually Francis and his companions formed the Franciscan order, which spread throughout Western Europe and gained more than 5,000 members in just a few years. Francis met (Saint) Clare of Assisi during this time and helped her found the female branch of the order.

Francis had a special connection with nature and animals. He talked to "brother sun" and "sister moon," he preached to flocks of birds, and he tamed a wolf that was killing people in a nearby town.

During his lifetime, Francis suffered from a number of illnesses, but he never complained. One day, after seeing a vision of Christ on the cross, he received the stigmata — the wounds of Christ — on his own hands, feet, and side.

In the last years of his life, Francis withdrew from the world and wrote his most famous work, *The Canticle of Brother Sun*. Francis died at age forty-five, half-blind and severely ill, and was canonized just a few years later.

Patron: Assisi, animals, the environment, the blind

1194–1253

AUGUST 11

Clare, the daughter of a wealthy family from Assisi, was so inspired by a sermon given by (Saint) Francis that she vowed to follow his way of life. Late one night, she secretly went to see Francis. In front of the altar, she dedicated herself to a life of poverty and vowed to become a Bride of Christ. She was eighteen years old.

Clare's parents were angry and insisted that she return home. Instead, Clare convinced her two sisters to join her. They lived in a small house near the church in Assisi. The sisters ate no meat, wore no shoes, and lived solely on donations. Anything extra they received was given to the needy.

Clare's faith and spiritual presence was contagious, and many women were drawn to follow her example. With assistance from Francis, Clare founded an order of nuns called the Poor Clares, named for their vow of extreme poverty. When the pope attempted to soften that vow, Clare responded: "How can a heart which possesses the infinite God be truly called poor?"

Clare shared Francis's love of nature and spent a great deal of time in the convent garden. The life of her order was filled with prayer, contemplation, and quiet. Despite a chronic illness that caused constant pain, Clare was ever cheerful and nurturing to the nuns in her care.

One morning Clare was so ill she could not attend church. While in bed, she received a vision and saw and heard the entire service. Because of this miracle, she was named patroness of television in 1985. She died at age fifty-nine and was canonized in 1255.

Patroness: embroiderers, television, eye diseases

Saint Thomas Aquinas

1225–1274
JANUARY 28

Born in a castle, Thomas was the son of a wealthy count who sent him to study with Benedictine monks when he was just five years old. Though classmates nicknamed him "the dumb ox" because he was large and quiet, Thomas was studying the philosophy of Plato and Aristotle at the University of Paris when he was fourteen.

After a few years, Thomas secretly joined the Dominican order. His prosperous family was not pleased by his vow of poverty and sent his two brothers to kidnap him. They locked Thomas in a tower, but he managed to escape a year later with the help of his sister.

Thomas returned to his studies, first in Italy, then in Paris, remaining in the Dominican order. Upon graduation, Thomas was ordained as a priest and taught theology at the University of Paris. During this time, he began to publish his writings. Thomas composed most of his works in his head and then dictated to secretaries, often to three or four at once! His greatest work, the *Summa Theologica*, is the foundation of modern Catholic doctrine. Though unfinished, it contains over two million words.

One year, on the feast of Saint Nicholas, Thomas experienced a powerful mystical vision. He never wrote again, explaining that all he had written was like straw compared to what he had seen in his vision. He died three months later. Thomas was canonized in 1323 and declared a Doctor of the Church in 1567.

Patron: academics, publishers, booksellers, theologians, Catholic schools and universities

Saint Bridget of Sweden

1302–1373
JULY 23

When she was only seven years old, Bridget had a vision of the Virgin Mary — the first of a lifetime of mystical visions and revelations. When she was thirteen, Bridget agreed to an arranged marriage, and she and her husband joined the lay order of Saint Francis. The couple raised eight children.

Bridget was considered a pious and charitable woman, and was called upon to serve Queen Blanche of Sweden as her chief lady-in-waiting. Although many palace workers mocked her as a result of her visions, Bridget counseled both the king and the queen for a number of years, and wrote down all of the revelations she received during this time.

After twenty-eight years of marriage, Bridget's husband died, and she left the court for a simpler life of Christian charity. She tended to the sick and poor near a Cistercian monastery, and many believed that Bridget possessed the powers of prophecy and miraculous healing.

Bridget enlisted the help of the king to found a community for monks and nuns, who would live separately but share the same church. She traveled to Rome in 1349 to obtain papal approval for her order.

As she waited, Bridget had the Bible translated into Swedish. She continued to care for the sick and needy, ate and slept very little, and spent much of her time in prayer. After many long years, her order received approval. The order, called the Brigittines, still exists today. Bridget died at the age of seventy-one, on the exact day she foretold. She was canonized in 1391.

Patroness: Sweden, Europe, widows, healers

Saint Catherine of Siena

1347–1380
APRIL 29

Catherine began to have mystical visions at a young age, including the ability to see guardian angels. When she was sixteen she joined the lay order of Saint Dominic, which allowed its members to remain in their own homes. She lived secluded in her bedroom, speaking to no one but her confessor for three years.

Finally, after a vision from Christ that instructed her to go out into the world, Catherine left home and began to tend to the sick and dying.

The radiance and wisdom Catherine obtained from her prayers and visions attracted many followers. She even started preaching in public, which was shocking to many people, because at that time, preaching was a man's job. Catherine's gift of speech was so powerful that four priests were needed to hear confessions after her sermons.

Though she preached often, Catherine also maintained a strong prayer life. In 1374, after praying at length in an ecstatic state, Catherine seemed for many hours to have died. Later, she said that Christ had commanded her to return to the world "for the good of souls."

Catherine had no formal education and could not write, so she dictated all her letters and treatises. Her most famous work, called *The Dialogue*, details her mystical conversations with Christ. Catherine's works are considered to be among the greatest theological writings of the Middle Ages.

When Catherine died at age thirty-three, the marks of the stigmata and the appearance of a wedding band (signifying her marriage to Christ) appeared on her body. She was canonized in 1461 and named a Doctor of the Church in 1970.

Patroness: Italy, nurses, the dying

Saint Joan of Arc

1412–1431
MAY 30

Joan was born into a peasant family in France during the Hundred Years' War between France and England. She was raised as a Christian but had no formal education. At age thirteen, Joan said she heard the voices of various saints telling her she had been chosen to help save France. Joan argued that she had no military training, but the voices gave her no peace. When she was seventeen, Joan dressed as a man and went to the commander of the French forces.

At first she had no success in convincing him to let her lead troops. Then she made a number of accurate predictions about upcoming battles. The commander sent Joan to speak to the prince of France, who had devised some tests for her. When Joan first arrived, he disguised himself and she easily picked him out of a crowd. Then she told him a secret about himself that no one else could know. Convinced, the prince ordered a suit of armor for Joan, and she was given a small army.

Carrying a banner emblazoned with the words "Jesus" and "Mary," Joan led the French army to defeat the English at Orleans. More victories followed, and Joan stood by the prince's side when he was crowned king of France. But shortly thereafter, jealous men of the court turned the king against Joan, and when she was captured and sold to the English, the king sent no rescue party.

The English put Joan on trial in Paris as a heretic and a witch, and she was burned at the stake when she was nineteen years old. Twenty years later her case was reopened and she was declared innocent of all charges. She was canonized in 1920.

Patroness: France, Orleans, soldiers, broadcasting, captives

Saint Bernardino of Siena

1380–1444
MAY 20

Sometimes called "the Apostle of Italy," Bernardino was orphaned at age six and raised by pious aunts. A terrible plague struck Italy when Bernardino was a young man, and he and twelve friends took over the administration of a local hospital. Bernardino cared for the sick night and day, and was himself bedridden for four months.

After he recovered, Bernardino received a vision that encouraged him to care for people's souls as well as their bodies. So he gave away all of his possessions, joined the Franciscan monks, and was ordained as a priest at age twenty-two. At first Bernardino did little preaching, for he had a weak, hoarse voice. After twelve years he was sent to Milan on a mission. He discovered that his voice had become strong and clear.

Preaching became Bernardino's calling. He walked all over Italy, giving many sermons each day. His words drew huge crowds and he could make people laugh and cry in turn. Bernardino had a plaque carved with the letters IHS (the Greek abbreviation for Jesus), which he often showed at the end of his sermons. He would invite the crowd to contemplate the Holy Name of Jesus. Some called this practice superstitious and denounced him to the pope, but Bernardino was found innocent of any wrongdoing.

Bernardino was so dedicated to his calling that even when he knew he was dying, he continued to preach for fifty-five days in a row. Bernardino was sixty-four years old when he died, and he was canonized in 1450.

Patron: Italy, advertising, respiratory problems

Saint Rita of Cascia

1381–1457
MAY 22

As a young girl, Rita visited a convent of Augustinian nuns in Cascia, Italy, and hoped to join them one day. Instead, her parents arranged her marriage and Rita was married at age twelve.

The next several years were difficult. Rita's husband had a violent temper, and her two sons took after him. As a result of extreme rivalry between two families in the city, Rita's husband was murdered. Her sons vowed retribution, but Rita prayed the boys would not have blood on their hands. Before they could take their revenge, they both died unexpectedly.

After their deaths, Rita again felt the call to religious life and applied to the Augustinian convent. At first she was denied because some of the nuns were related to the family that had murdered her husband. But she was permitted to join the convent after working to heal the rift between the rivals.

For the next forty years Rita devoted herself to a spiritual life of prayer and service. She often prayed in front of an image of the crucifixion, and one day as she was meditating, a small wound appeared on her forehead, as if she had been struck by one of the thorns from the crown on Christ's head. This wound remained with her for the rest of her life.

Rita was ill and confined to her bed for several years before her death. Her holiness attracted many visitors, and she remained cheerful through her suffering. Once, she asked a visitor to bring her a rose from her parents' house. Though it was January, her impossible request was granted: a single rose was found blossoming on the bush. Rita was canonized in 1900.

Patroness: abuse victims, widows, impossible causes

Saint Angela Mereci

1470–1540
JANUARY 27

Angela was a prayerful, devout young girl. She was drawn to stories about the saints and wanted to imitate their lives. When she was old enough, Angela joined a group called the Third Order of Saint Francis, which allowed her to live at home.

Her greatest desire was to teach children, especially girls, who in those days were not educated unless they were rich or became nuns. So Angela left the order, gathered a group of unmarried women, and began traveling from house to house to teach impoverished girls. The group took Saint Ursula as their patron but did not take full vows to become nuns, because they wanted to live and work among the people instead of remaining secluded in a convent.

In 1524, on her way to visit the Holy Land, Angela was struck with sudden blindness. She continued her journey, saying she only needed to see with her spiritual eyes and heart. On the return trip, her sight was miraculously restored at the same place where she had lost it.

Soon after her return, the pope requested that Angela take charge of an order of nuns dedicated to nursing the sick, but Angela was so sure of her calling to educate poor girls that she turned down the appointment.

Angela died in 1540, but the Company of Saint Ursula continued to grow. Although it was never a religious order in her lifetime, the Ursulines were the first group of religious women to work outside the convent, and the first teaching order of women. Today, the Ursuline Sisters are active in countries all over the world. Angela was canonized in 1807.

Patroness: illness, loss of parents, the disabled, the handicapped

Saint Juan Diego

1474–1548

DECEMBER 9

Juan Diego was born to a poor Aztec family in Mexico. One morning on his way to church, Juan heard angelic music coming from somewhere nearby. He looked around and saw a beautiful woman dressed like an Aztec princess, surrounded by a brilliant light at the top of a hill.

The woman identified herself as the Virgin Mary and told Juan to call her "Our Lady of Guadalupe." She said she wanted a church built where they were standing so that his people could come to know "her Mother's heart," and that she would console all who came to her with sorrows.

Juan went to the bishop with what he had seen, but the bishop did not take Juan seriously. The next day, Juan met the Lady in the same spot, and he begged her to pick someone of greater social standing to convince the bishop. She replied that she had chosen him, and urged him to go to the bishop once more.

The bishop, still doubtful, asked for proof that the woman Juan had seen was indeed the Virgin Mary. Juan once again went to the hillside, but when he arrived, the Lady was not there. There instead, although it was the middle of winter, was a rosebush in full bloom. Juan gathered the flowers in his cloak and brought them to the bishop. As flowers tumbled out of Juan's cloak, the bishop's surprise became amazement. For on the cloak itself, in glowing colors, was a full-length picture of the Lady.

The church was built, and Juan's cloak with the image of Our Lady of Guadalupe has remained in perfect condition in the church to this day. Juan Diego was canonized in 2002.

Patron: Our Lady of Guadalupe

Saint Francis Xavier

1506–1552

DECEMBER 3

Francis was born into a noble Spanish family and planned to become a professor. While studying at the University of Paris, however, he met (Saint) Ignatius of Loyola, who persuaded Francis to dedicate his life to God.

The two men founded the Society of Jesus (also called Jesuits), whose members were committed to missionary work and education. Francis was sent to Goa, India, where he tended to people in hospitals and prisons and taught catechism classes to children and slaves. He traveled barefoot, lived mainly on rice and water, and gained a reputation as a healer and miracle worker.

Francis then set his sights on spreading the gospel to Japan. The Japanese did not take him seriously in his poor, barefoot state so he changed his tactics and his garments. Well-dressed, he presented himself as a representative of Portugal and brought gifts to a local ruler. Soon he was allowed to use a vacant Buddhist monastery for services. In a short time Francis converted thousands of Japanese people to Christianity.

Francis returned to India to monitor the progress of the missionaries he had trained to continue his work. His next goal was China, a country closed to foreigners. He planned a secret entry into the country but became ill on the journey and died near Hong Kong. According to some accounts, Francis baptized more than 40,000 people in India, the East Indies, and Japan. He was canonized in 1622.

Patron: China, the East Indies, India, Japan, foreign missions

Saint Ignatius of Loyola

1491–1556
JULY 31

Ignatius was born in Spain to noble parents. When he was old enough, Ignatius joined the army, but before he had served very long he was severely wounded in the leg by a cannonball.

While recovering from surgery, Ignatius asked for something to read to relieve his boredom. He wanted adventure novels, but instead was given stories about the life of Christ and the lives of the saints. Ignatius was inspired by these stories and soon converted. He began writing down ways to help himself combat discouragement and worldly temptation, which became his best-known work, *Spiritual Exercises*.

When he was well enough to travel, Ignatius went to the Holy Land and there became convinced he needed to start a new order, an "Army of God," that would spread the gospel around the world. He returned home and went back to school, studying with little children to make up for a poor childhood education. Finally, he attended the University of Paris.

There he met Francis Xavier, and together they formed the Society of Jesus, or Jesuits, whose main goal was to preach the gospel around the world. Ignatius was elected the head of this society and served in this capacity until his death at the age of sixty-five.

At the time of his death, over 1,500 Jesuits were teaching the gospel in thirty-five colleges and schools in eleven countries. Ignatius was canonized in 1609.

Patron: spiritual exercises, many schools and colleges

Saint Teresa of Avila

1515–1582
OCTOBER 15

Born in Spain, Teresa was strong-willed and eccentric. As a young girl, she wanted to run off to Morocco with her brother to die as a martyr. When she was a teenager, Teresa began reading the letters of Saint Jerome and was inspired to join religious life. Her father opposed this idea, but Teresa ran away from home to become a nun.

The Carmelite order Teresa joined was more like a social club than a place of prayer. Many nuns wore jewelry, entertained visitors, and came and went as they pleased. Teresa was popular, and she found it hard to pray with all the distractions.

Then she contracted a severe illness, which paralyzed her legs for three years. During this time, she focused on Christ, prayed intensely, and began to have mystical visions and ecstasies. According to one account, her body sometimes actually rose off the ground while she prayed!

When she was forty-three, Teresa founded a stricter order of Carmelites who took more seriously their vows of poverty, prayer, and seclusion. Teresa's order was called the Discalced (which means "barefoot") Carmelites, and she enlisted Saint John of the Cross to form a group of Discalced monks. Teresa was harshly criticized by other religious orders for being too strict, but she never weakened her resolve.

Teresa spent much time writing about her mystical experiences; her best-known works are *The Interior Castle* and *The Way of Perfection*. Teresa died at age sixty-seven, and her body has remained miraculously preserved. She was canonized in 1622 and is the first woman to be named a Doctor of the Church.

Patroness: bodily ills, headaches, sickness, Spain, people ridiculed for their piety

Saint Charles Borromeo

1538–1584
NOVEMBER 4

Charles was born to a wealthy, noble family in Italy. By age twenty-two, he had obtained doctoral degrees in both civil and Church law.

A year later, Charles's uncle was appointed Pope Pius IV, and Charles was named Secretary of State in Rome. Though he would have preferred the quiet life of a monk, Charles worked tirelessly for the papal court.

During this time, the progress of the Protestant Reformation and accusations of abuse within the Church were weakening the Catholic Church. In response, Charles helped reopen the Council of Trent, which sought to reform abuses, enforce stricter discipline of Church leaders, and better educate Catholics about their faith.

In accordance with the decrees of the Council, he helped build new seminaries, improved Catholic worship and music books, and organized Sunday schools for children. In 1563, Charles was ordained as a priest, and a year later he was appointed Bishop of Milan.

He continued to help better the Catholic Church. He drafted the Catechism and created the Confraternity of Christian Doctrine (CCD) classes that continue to be held today.

Despite his hard work, some clergymen were upset with Charles's enforcement of strict discipline, and they attempted to kill him. Charles was fired upon at close range, but was not hit.

Throughout his life, Charles raised money for needy families and tended to the sick and dying. He was canonized in 1610.

Patron: apple orchards, colic, bishops, catechists, seminarians

Saint John of the Cross

1542–1591

When he was fourteen years old, John worked as a nurse's aide at a local hospital in Spain, where he learned compassion for the sick and the poor. He attended a Jesuit college and joined religious life in a Carmelite order after graduation.

John was ordained in 1567 and shortly thereafter met (Saint) Teresa of Avila. She urged him to help reform the Carmelite order, and John, sympathetic to the idea of a return to the older rule of poverty and contemplation, established a monastery where strict rule was enforced. These monks, like their female counterparts, were called Discalced (Barefoot).

After a few years, John became the spiritual director at Teresa's convent. John and Teresa were unpopular for their strict rule, and John was kidnapped by monks from his own order. He was imprisoned in a cold cell with a tiny window so high he could not look out. Although he was beaten routinely and given only bread and water to eat, John composed beautiful mystical poetry about his union with God during this time. His most famous work is called *Dark Night of the Soul*.

Nine months later, John managed to escape. He returned to his community and continued to work for reform in the Carmelite order until finally Church authorities split the Carmelites into two groups, the Calced (those who wear shoes) and the Discalced.

John lived in peace for several years, writing and preaching, but toward the end of his life, John again endured persecution. After Teresa died, the Catholic Church stripped John of his leadership and banished him from the monastery. He died in exile at the age of forty-nine. He was canonized in 1726 and became a Doctor of the Church in 1926.

Patron: poets, contemplatives, mystics

Saint Rose of Lima

1586–1617
AUGUST 30

Rose was born in Lima, Peru, the first saint born in the New World. Her birth name was Isabel, but because she was so beautiful, her parents changed her name to Rose. When she was just five years old, Rose declared that she would marry no man but Christ himself.

When she got older, Rose's good looks attracted many young men. To discourage their advances, she tried to make herself less attractive by rubbing hot pepper and lime onto her face and hands. Rose decided to become a nun, and she chose an order that did not require her to live in a convent.

Rose sold vegetables she grew and pieces of embroidery she sewed to help support her family and others in need. She also set up an infirmary in her parents' home and cared for orphans, the sick, and the elderly.

For most of her life, however, Rose stayed alone in a small shed in her parents' garden, where she could commune with Christ and the Blessed Virgin uninterrupted. Rose believed that the more she suffered as Christ had suffered, the closer she would become to him. She denied herself all but the tiniest amount of food and drink, and she devised penances for herself, like wearing studded chains around her waist and a crown of iron spikes under her veil. Rose's family and her priest attempted to stop these practices, but they were not successful.

While enduring such extreme self-inflicted torture, Rose was amazingly cheerful. Many people who saw her said she looked radiant, and some considered her a living saint. She died at age thirty-one and was canonized in 1671.

Patroness: florists, gardeners, Peru, South America

Saint Francis de Sales

1567–1622

Francis knew from a young age that he wanted to become a priest. His parents, however, wanted him to become a lawyer, so he agreed to study law. But eventually he could no longer ignore his spiritual calling and was ordained as a priest. Francis soon gained a reputation as a wonderful preacher and was sent from his native France to Geneva, Switzerland, to convert Calvinists who had left the Catholic faith.

Francis was met with harsh words and stones, but bore the abuse patiently. When few people came to hear his sermons, he distributed hand-written leaflets under doors to get his message across. Surviving years of difficulties — and even an attempt on his life — Francis, with his gentle style of preaching, succeeded in converting thousands of people.

In 1602, Francis was appointed bishop of Geneva. During this time, he met (Saint) Jeanne de Chantal, a widow, and became her spiritual director. Under Francis's guidance, she founded the Order of the Visitation for women who wanted to serve God without the requirement of living in a convent.

One of Francis's core beliefs was that any person could achieve holiness. In 1608, he composed the *Introduction to the Devout Life*, a devotional for ordinary people. Francis urged all Christians, clergy and laity alike, to lead spiritual lives of prayer and good works.

Francis wore himself out with constant travel and died at the age of fifty-five. He was canonized in 1662 and named a Doctor of the Church in 1877.

Patron: writers, the Catholic press, the hearing-impaired

Saint Martin de Porres

1579–1639
NOVEMBER 3

Born in Lima, Peru, Martin was the illegitimate son of a Spanish nobleman and a free black woman. Raised by his mother, Martin grew up in poverty and was outcast and ridiculed for his mixed blood. His compassion for the poor and needy grew when he was apprenticed to a barber/surgeon. At that time, this profession combined hair-cutting with surgical and medical skills.

Since at that time a non-white had no prospect of being ordained, Martin joined the Dominican order as a layperson. Cheerful and humble, he worked in the kitchen, laundry, garden, and infirmary in exchange for room and board.

Martin served the people of Lima, too, helping to set up an orphanage and caring for the sick during a plague. He was especially concerned with the health and welfare of the slaves, Indians, and other people who were considered of little worth to society.

Martin helped travelers by planting fruit trees along the road, and many times offered his own bed to immigrants while they were looking for work. His compassion extended to animals; he even set up a shelter for abandoned cats and dogs.

Martin quickly gained a reputation as a healer and holy man. Even bishops sought his advice and healing gifts. According to one story, the Archbishop of Mexico claimed Martin cured him of a disease with a touch of his hands. After his death, many miraculous cures were reported at his tomb. He was canonized in 1962.

Patron: racial harmony

Saint Vincent de Paul

1581–1660
SEPTEMBER 27

Born into a poor French family, Vincent chose to join the priesthood as a way to earn money. Shortly after he was ordained, Vincent was captured by pirates while returning home from a trip and sold as a slave. His true conversion took place after he escaped.

Upon his return to France, Vincent began the work for which he is most famous: charity for the poor. He began working as a tutor and confessor for a wealthy family and was able to inspire them to help fund many charitable organizations. With their donations, Vincent established hospitals, orphanages, and soup kitchens. He worked to improve conditions for prisoners and slaves. Vincent was a gentleman in society, and at the same time a friend of tradesmen and the poor. People from all walks of life were drawn by his charismatic personality and dedication to serving others.

Vincent also founded religious institutes in areas where there was little education, and he taught his "little method," a preaching style that was clear and easy to understand. Members of Vincent's order, the Congregation of the Mission, traveled all over France, the British Isles, Poland, and Italy.

He also helped (Saint) Louise de Marillac found the Sisters of Charity. This group of noncloistered nuns became an important force in providing hospital care for the poor.

Since Vincent's death in 1660, his body has remained miraculously preserved to this day. In 1833, the St. Vincent de Paul Society, a Catholic charitable organization dedicated to serving people in need, was founded in Vincent's honor. Vincent was canonized in 1737.

Patron: charities, hospitals, volunteers, prisoners

Saint Louise de Marillac

1591–1660

MARCH 15

Louise was raised by her father, a French aristocrat, and educated at a Dominican convent. When she was fifteen, her father died and Louise married Anthony Le Gras, who was then secretary to the Queen of France. Louise socialized with many rich and powerful people, but was also keenly interested in helping the poor. A born leader and organizer, Louise guided her wealthy friends in charity work for the poor.

After her husband's death in 1625, Louise met (Saint) Vincent de Paul, who became her spiritual advisor. The two shared an interest in organizing a group of women to serve the poor in parishes all over France. Louise traveled around the country to learn what services were most needed, and she set up structures to help volunteers organize and serve efficiently in each community.

When Louise returned to Paris, she formed a small community of young women whom she trained to assist the poor in the city. This community became the Daughters of Charity. For the first ten years, the women took no formal vows, and after that they took vows for one year only, renewing each year as they felt called. The Daughters of Charity were not cloistered in a convent, but rather ministered in streets, hospitals, orphanages, and schools. Louise urged them to see the image of Christ in each person they helped.

Because of Louise's vision, there are 25,000 Daughters of Charity serving throughout the world today. She was canonized in 1934.

Patroness: social workers

Blessed Kateri Tekakwitha

1656–1680
JULY 14

Kateri's mother was a Christian Algonquin and her father was an Iroquois. Both died of smallpox when Kateri was only four, and she was raised by her uncle, a Mohawk chief. Though Kateri survived the plague, she was severely disfigured and almost blind as a result.

Kateri had no formal religious education, but she remembered her mother's strong faith and often went to the woods to talk to God. She was overjoyed when a Jesuit missionary opened a chapel near her village in what is now New York state.

Her uncle did not like the Jesuit priest, but finally gave his consent for Kateri to learn about Christianity. When she was twenty-one, Kateri was baptized. Her family and her people did not accept her choice, however, and Kateri suffered beatings, and stoning and death threats. Because she would not work on Sundays, she was not allowed to eat that day. Soon she had to flee for her life.

Kateri traveled 200 miles on foot through the wilderness and finally reached the mission of St. Francis Xavier near Montreal. There she led the life she desired, praying continually and helping the poor and the sick. Kateri's favorite place was still the forest. She fashioned crosses out of sticks and placed them in different locations, making her own natural Stations of the Cross. Even in winter, she would kneel out in the snow to pray.

Kateri vowed never to marry and hoped to start a convent for Native American Sisters. But, weakened by poor health, Kateri died when she was twenty-four. Her last words were "Jesus, I love you." In 1980 the Catholic Church declared Kateri "Blessed."

Patroness: ecology and the environment, World Youth Day

Saint John Baptist de La Salle

1651–1719
APRIL 7

John Baptist grew up in France in a time of war, political turmoil, and extreme separation between rich and poor classes. Though John Baptist was born into a wealthy family and had the benefit of a good education, there were no schools at all for poor children.

He studied for the priesthood and was appointed as a clergyman for a cathedral in Rheims. Then he met Adrien Nyel, a layman who had opened four free schools for poor boys. Together they opened two schools in Rheims, and John Baptist began his lifelong vocation of educating boys. He resigned as clergyman and gave all of his money to the poor.

At first John Baptist was not pleased with the teaching methods used in his schools. In order to better train the teachers, he invited them to come and live in his house. His family was not pleased with this arrangement, so eventually John Baptist rented quarters for the teachers and moved out to join them. He decided to found an order of laymen, the Brothers of the Christian Schools. He did not want any of the Brothers to take religious orders because he wanted their entire attention to be focused on learning how to teach.

John Baptist was responsible for drastic changes in the teaching methods of the time. He ordered that reading be taught in French instead of in the customary Latin, so that young students could learn to read faster in their spoken language. He was the first to create teaching by grade, with a number of students in each class, instead of individual tutoring. Before he died, John Baptist opened free schools for all social classes, a reform school for troubled boys, and Sunday school classes in Paris. He was canonized in 1900.

Patron: schoolteachers

Saint Elizabeth Ann Seton

1774–1821
JANUARY 4

Elizabeth grew up in a wealthy family in New York City. Raised as an Episcopalian, she grew up with the love of Scriptures. At age twenty, Elizabeth married William Seton, a wealthy merchant, and the couple had five children. After they had been married nine years, William's business failed and his health along with it. While the Setons were in Italy seeking a cure for his tuberculosis, William died.

Elizabeth had always been interested in the Catholic faith, and she converted upon her return to the United States. An intelligent and resourceful woman, Elizabeth opened a boardinghouse in New York and worked a number of other jobs to support her children.

Inspired by the life of Saint Vincent de Paul, Elizabeth founded the first religious community in the United States, the American Sisters of Charity, in 1809. Elizabeth and eighteen sisters took their vows, and she became known as Mother Seton from that time on. The Sisters were devoted to serving the poor and teaching in schools and orphanages.

Mother Seton opened the first parochial school, which became a model for the parochial school system throughout the United States.

At the time of her death there were many communities of Sisters in North and South America, as well as in Italy, and the American Sisters of Charity continue to serve to this day. Elizabeth was canonized in 1975.

Patroness: widows, the loss of parents

Saint Catherine Laboure

1806–1876
NOVEMBER 28

Catherine is known for her visions. When she was a teenager, Catherine said she had a dream during which Saint Vincent de Paul appeared to her and encouraged her to join the Daughters of Charity in Paris. In 1830, she joined the order.

While a novice there, Catherine received a number of remarkable visions of the Virgin Mary. In one vision, Catherine saw Mary standing on a globe of the world with streams of light coming from her hands. She heard a voice saying, "These rays are the graces that Mary obtains for men." Then golden letters appeared in a semicircle around the figure, forming the words: "O Mary, conceived without sin, pray for us who have recourse to thee." The figure turned around and Catherine saw the letter *M* with a cross above it, while below it were the hearts of Mary and Jesus. After the vision, Catherine heard a voice urging that a medal be created from these images, and that whoever carried the medal would be given special protection by the Mother of God.

Catherine kept her visions a secret from everyone except Father Aladel, her confessor. Through his efforts and the permission of the archbishop, the first 1,500 copies of a medal bearing the images from Catherine's visions were created. Use of the medal spread rapidly, and, because of its wonderworking power, it earned the name "The Miraculous Medal."

For many years after her vision, Catherine cared for dying patients and worked in the kitchen at a hospice. Shortly before her death, Catherine finally told one of her superiors about her visions. News of her secret traveled quickly, and when she died, great crowds came to venerate her. Catherine was canonized in 1947.

Patroness: the Miraculous Medal

Saint Bernadette

1844–1879
APRIL 16

Bernadette, a frail child who suffered from asthma, wanted to enter a convent but was refused because of her ill health. She helped support her poor family instead by tending sheep. One day while gathering firewood, fourteen-year-old Bernadette saw her first vision, known as the Apparition at Lourdes.

In a rocky cave, or grotto, she saw a beautiful woman dressed in blue and white, holding a rosary. Roses blossomed at her feet. The woman, who called herself "The Immaculate Conception," asked Bernadette to pray the rosary with her, and to have a chapel built in the grotto. After another vision, Bernadette began digging at the earth with her hands at the place the woman had instructed. In a few minutes water began to bubble up from a hidden spring.

When people heard what had happened, many followed Bernadette to the site of her visions, but only Bernadette was able to see the woman. Because of Bernadette's simple, quiet dignity, many people believed her. Others remained suspicious, however, and for years Bernadette was questioned about her visions of the Virgin Mary.

She eventually moved to a convent to avoid the attention, and she did not even attend the dedication when a church was built on the site of her visions. After suffering from tuberculosis for many years, Bernadette died. Her body has remained miraculously preserved since her death. She was canonized in 1933.

To this day thousands have reported miraculous healing from the water Bernadette found in the hidden spring. More than 200 million people have visited the shrine to the Virgin Mary at Lourdes. Next to Rome, it is the most popular pilgrimage site in Europe.

Patroness: Lourdes, France, shepherdesses, sick people

Saint Therese of Lisieux

1873–1897

OCTOBER 1

Born to a devout family in France, Therese was strong-willed and emotional. When she was eight years old, she became so ill that no one thought she would survive. Therese prayed to a statue of Mary, and when she saw the statue smile at her, she was miraculously cured.

Therese knew she wanted to become a nun, and she tried to join the Carmelites. The bishop denied her request because of her young age — she was only fifteen at the time. On a pilgrimage to Rome, Therese boldly spoke to the pope himself, begging to become a nun. Soon after, her wish was granted.

Therese joined the convent in Lisieux where two of her sisters already had taken their vows. When her older sister became prioress, she asked Therese to remain a novice. Some of the nuns felt Therese's family would otherwise have too much power within the convent. Therese happily made this sacrifice. She decided that the way to achieve holiness for a simple person like herself was to follow a "little way" filled with small sacrifices.

Ill health prevented Therese from fulfilling her dream to be a missionary, but for years she sent letters of encouragement to other foreign missionaries.

Therese is often called the "Little Flower," a name she took for herself. She saw herself as a small wildflower, simple and unnoticed by most, yet blossoming and glorifying God.

She believed that she would be more helpful to others after her death, and Therese promised her sisters that she would send a "shower of roses" upon anyone who asked for her aid. The "Little Flower" was just twenty-four years old when she died of tuberculosis. She was canonized in 1925.

Patroness: missionaries, florists, tuberculosis, illness

Saint Maximilian Kolbe

1894–1941
AUGUST 14

Born into a poor but pious Catholic family in Poland, Maximilian was considered wild and mischievous. His life changed during his first communion, when he was twelve. Maximilian saw a vision of the Virgin Mary and asked her for direction in his life. She showed him two crowns, one red and one white, and asked if he was willing to accept either crown. The white one meant that he should "persevere in purity," and the red that he would become a martyr. He accepted them both.

Maximilian entered seminary in Rome and founded the Knights of the Immaculate, an order devoted to Mary and the Miraculous medal and dedicated to spreading the gospel. Maximilian was ordained at age twenty-four and earned his Doctor of Theology four years later.

Returning to Poland to teach history in the Krakow seminary, Maximilian was stricken with bouts of tuberculosis that left him in poor health for the rest of his life. But this did not stop his plans. The monastery he founded grew to a community of 800. They published a magazine, *The Knight of the Immaculate*, which at its peak circulated 750,000 copies a month. Maximilian traveled to Japan and, within a month, was publishing the magazine in Japanese. The monastery he founded in Nagasaki still serves today as a center for Franciscan work.

In 1941, Maximilian was arrested in Poland by the Nazis for harboring Jewish refugees. He was sent to Auschwitz. When a prisoner escaped, ten men were chosen to die as an example, among them a married man with children. Maximilian volunteered to take his place. He was starved for three weeks and then executed. He was forty-seven years old and had earned both of his crowns. He was canonized in 1982.

Patron: political prisoners, the pro-life movement, journalists

Saint Katharine Drexel

1858–1955
MARCH 3

Born in Pennsylvania, Katharine learned about charity from her wealthy father and stepmother. Two days a week, she helped her stepmother distribute food, clothes, and money to the needy. Her father was extremely generous to many charities, and when he died Katharine continued in his footsteps.

Katharine became interested in the plight of the Native Americans living on reservations in the west. She wanted to see the conditions for herself, so Katharine traveled by stagecoach and even by donkey to make the journey. She spent great sums of her inheritance on setting up schools, funding teachers' salaries, and supplying basic needs of food and clothing for the Native Americans. She found priests to serve their spiritual needs, too. As she became aware of the plight of African Americans, especially in the South, Katharine generously supported the Bureau of Colored and Indian Missions.

She entered religious life in 1889, with the blessing of her lifelong friend and spiritual advisor, Bishop O'Connor. He encouraged Katharine to found a new order to serve the needs of African Americans and Native Americans. She and thirteen companions took vows in 1891 under the name of the Sisters of the Blessed Sacrament.

Mother Drexel, as she was now called, was responsible for establishing, staffing, and supporting nearly sixty schools and missions. She founded the only black Catholic college in the United States, Xavier University of Louisiana.

After suffering from a heart attack in 1935, Mother Drexel spent the last twenty years of her life in seclusion and prayer. She was canonized in 2000.

Patroness: South Louisiana, against racism, Xavier University of Louisiana

Saint Padre Pio

1887–1968
SEPTEMBER 23

Born in Italy, Padre Pio was gifted with visions from a young age. When he was fifteen, he joined the Capuchins, an order dedicated to poverty and prayer. One day he heard a voice telling him that he would receive the wounds of Christ, just as Saint Francis had.

In 1918, eight years after becoming a priest, he was praying in front of a crucifix and saw an unearthly light shining from the container of the Blessed Sacrament. Later, several friars found him unconscious on the floor, bleeding from wounds in his hands, side, and feet. For the next fifty years these wounds continued to bleed and never healed. Each day Padre Pio lost about a cup of blood and suffered a great deal of pain. Doctors were baffled by his condition.

Padre Pio's great calling was to hear people's confessions, which he did for more than ten hours a day. Often he knew what was in people's hearts before they spoke, and people waited for hours in long lines so that he might hear their confessions. When he served Mass, Padre Pio often wept and became transfixed, seeing visions that were not of this world.

Countless people reported that Padre Pio could cure hopeless illnesses, and many people claimed to have seen him, though he never left his monastery. During World War II, a number of pilots reported seeing the figure of a monk in the clouds and were unable to drop any bombs near Padre Pio's monastery.

Through fundraising efforts, Padre Pio founded a large hospital, the House for the Relief of Suffering, in Italy in 1958. He also started many prayer groups around the world that are still active today. Padre Pio died in 1968 and was canonized in 2002.

Patron: serenity, the sick

Blessed Teresa of Calcutta

1910–1997
SEPTEMBER 5

Born in Macedonia and baptized Gonxha Agnes, Mother Teresa adopted her name when she joined the missionary Sisters of Loreto in Ireland at age eighteen. They sent her to teach in Calcutta, India, at Saint Mary's School for girls, which she served for the next twenty years.

In 1946 Mother Teresa received a special "call within a call." Over the next weeks and months she saw visions during which Christ asked her to serve the poorest of the poor so that they might know his love. After two years of testing by Church authorities, Mother Teresa was given permission to establish the Missionaries of Charity.

Adopting a blue and white Indian sari for her habit, Mother Teresa began her lifelong dedication to caring for the sick among the poorest classes. After Mass each day, she went out into the streets of Calcutta and nursed those she called "the unwanted, the unloved, the uncared for," many of whom suffered from leprosy, AIDS, and other diseases. Many former students flocked to Mother Teresa's side — so many that she was able to send Sisters to all parts of India.

Over the next forty years Mother Teresa founded other missionary groups of brothers and priests, as well as groups of laypeople and volunteers from different faiths and nationalities. By the end of her life she had established over 600 foundations in 100 countries, with over 4,000 members serving the poor.

Mother Teresa received the Nobel Peace Prize in 1979, one in a long list of honors. Considered a living saint by many, Mother Teresa was declared "Blessed" by the Church just a few years after her death in 1997. In 2002, Pope John Paul II permitted the opening of her cause of canonization.

Patroness: Calcutta, the poor

Index of Saints

Glossary

Canonized: declared a saint

Clergy: a general name referring to a religious leader (like a priest or bishop)

Cloistered: enclosed; separated from the outside world. Convents, where nuns reside, and monasteries, where monks live, are cloistered.

Doctor of the Church: a special title given by the Church to a saint whose writings, preaching, and theological understanding are deemed useful to Christians "in any age of the Church"

Ecstatic: a supernatural state during which a person focuses on a religious subject so intensely that the activity of the five senses is suspended

Heretic: someone baptized in the Catholic Church who outright denies a truth or doctrine of the faith

Layperson/Laity: a member or members of a religious community who are not clergy

Martyr: a person who accepts death for refusing to renounce his or her faith

Mystic: someone who believes in the existence of realities beyond human comprehension

Order: organization in which people live under a common Rule, such as poverty, chastity, and obedience

Rule: plan of life and discipline approved by the government of the church which members of a religious order vow to live in accordance with